Pointing at the Pachyderms

Selected Lyrics 1978 to 2013

Ian McGregor

Cover design and wonderful pictures by
Ian Smith

ISBN 978-1-291-33366-4

www.ianmcgregor.co.uk

Introduction

I hadn't made up my mind whether to include an introduction and also whether to include notes about individual lyrics. In a project which already smacks a little of vanity publishing, would the inclusion of these be a massage for the ego? Well, what if it is? My ego has been bruised often enough and so a gentle massage would do no harm!

And then I got "Mother, Brother, Lover" by Jarvis Cocker out of the library. And it had both an introduction and extensive notes, both of which enhanced my enjoyment and appreciation of the book (as well as confirming Jarvis Cocker as one of my favourite lyricists – very near the top of the growing list of those who were born later than me). So the matter was settled.

Then, just before I started writing this introduction, I heard on the news about the death of Hal David, best known as the lyricist for much of the Burt Bacharach catalogue. Looking into that, I discovered just how many great lyrics Hal David had written. You know some of them – I guarantee it.

As the sub title suggests, this little book is a collection of lyrics which I have written (or, in a couple of cases, co-written) over the past 35 years. There are a number of exclusions which would have been worth their place but are not here because I couldn't find them! The main category is my first songwriting partnership, with David Goldman; I have a folder somewhere – probably at the back and bottom of a large walk in cupboard. (It would be walk in but for how full it is)! One day perhaps.

The lyrics for the songs with David were written between about 1974 to 1978; between the ages of 18 and 22 if you, like me, find that an interesting detail. However, even if you don't find that interesting, that is when they were written. I look forward to finding these. From what I can remember, there were some rather interesting stories behind the songs and memories prompted by them. For example "Postcard from Dusseldorf" which was based on an incident at work where an old man showed me a postcard of (can you guess where?) and said something like "Who won the war?" and was bemoaning the beautiful modern city. Of course, part of the reason for it being like that is that the Allies flattened it during the war and there was no option but to rebuild. Dusseldorf has loomed large in my music listening over the years being the home city of Kraftwerk; "When I press down a little key, it plays a little melody." Or, in the as yet unreleased "Kraftwerk Unplugged", "When I press down a little key, it goes 'click'."

So that leaves me with the lyrics contained herein. I have left one or two out because they are substandard. (You may be of the opinion that I set the bar too low on that one)!

I have always loved lyrics, both as an integral part of many songs, and most great songs, and also in their own right. Sometimes, lyrics that sound great are exposed as of very little literary merit when set out on the page. A prime example would be the lyrics of one of my earliest (and continuing) influences – Marc Bolan of T. Rex. Some of his are almost devoid of meaning in themselves - but the sound of them is great. And that is a lesson that has stayed with me.

Not sure where I am going with this introduction. Perhaps mentioning some of my other favourite lyricists would be useful. When I was 15 and really starting to get "into" music, my two favourite bands were Fairport Convention and T. Rex. The latter was deeply embarrassing to admit to at my (all male) school and the other was suitably obscure but critically revered. As mentioned, Marc Bolan's lyrics were, and are, special to me. However, the Fairport school and the lyrics of their songs were more important. As well as pointing to contemporary songwriting greats like Dylan and Joni Mitchell, they mined the catalogue of traditional song and especially ballads which have been influential. But Fairport also had, and indeed have, some fine songwriters. Sandy Denny and Richard Thompson are rightly highly regarded. However, I would also rate Dave Swarbrick, who is underrated as a writer, Ashley Hutchings who hit a rich vein of very literary songwriting in his middle years, and now Chris Leslie who has brought some excellent songs to the band in the past decade and more with some distinctly unusual subject matter.

Leonard Cohen of course. Pete Townshend. The late great Larry Norman ("Why should the devil have all the good music?"). The lyrical half of songwriting partnerships.

Clive James who wrote some amazing lyrics for Pete Atkin. Joe Strummer who leant more to lyrics while Mick Jones leant more to music in The Clash. And, possibly top of that list, William Schwenck Gilbert. Yes – W.S. Gilbert of Gilbert & Sullivan.

And I almost forgot to mention the late great Jackie Leven and the not late – and great – Michael Weston King.

I admit it - I am not a poet. I occasionally write poetry and maybe one day I might dare to call myself a poet. However, my forte appears to be lyrics and I do have, I think, a facility for rhymes. In fact, I find it difficult to write without rhymes forcing their way in – for example

> The real poet told me
> "Poems don't need rhymes."
> I said "That's true
> They just do –
> Sometimes."

Without even trying, I had subconsciously gone into rhyming mode.

I have enjoyed writing the notes and hope that they are of some interest to the reader. My interpretations of the lyrics are not definitive. If you find a meaning that speaks to you, so be it. I will be delighted that it has spoken to you at all, even if it doesn't necessarily convey what I meant to say. In one or two cases, I have not got a clue what the lyric means so it is completely open season on those.

Thanks to

Collaborators (in order of first appearance in book) –

Elaine McGregor, David Barron, Dougie Nicol, Peter Bloomfield, Sybil Maguire, Helen Macalan, Ronnie Blair. All of the contents of this book are, at least potentially, songs. Most have tunes, others may yet have tunes.

Informers (in order of first appearance in book) –

Rachel Chown, Ken & Marjorie Brown, Julyan Lidstone, Stuart McGregor, Carole McGregor, Ian Smith, Jim Borland, Stephen Vance, Ellie Avanelle, Elaine McGregor, David McGregor, Stella Howell, Isla McGregor, Samantha's sister, the Scottish Fellowship of Christian Writers, Billy Kent, Johnny Holms, Heather Innes, Jim Gourlay, Raymond Muirhead, John Wallace, Helenora Smith, Ann(e) Clark.

Dedicated to –

Carole McGregor

Pointing at the Pachyderm

You can't ignore an elephant;
It takes up too much space.
You can't squeeze it in a cupboard
And then vacuum up each trace.
You can't live inside a bubble
Cut off from every germ.
I think it's time for pointing -
Pointing at the pachyderm.

There's an elephant in the room.
There's an elephant in the room.
It's not leaving any time soon.
There's an elephant in the room.

You can show God your anger;
He knows it anyway.
Even before you think it,
He knows what you will say.
Three score years and ten
Cut down to a shorter term.
I think it's time for pointing -
Pointing at the pachyderm.

You can't fail to mention dying
To the terminally ill.
You might think they'll thank you;
But I don't think they will.
You both believe in heaven -
So why don't you both affirm.
I think it's time for pointing -
Pointing at the pachyderm.

It's reminding me of Lewis -
"The Last Battle" and beyond.
"A Grief Observed" is painful
Yet we somehow carry on.
Looking forward to the holidays,
Waiting for the end of term.
I think it's time for pointing -
Pointing at the pachyderm.

Illness isn't funny;
Unless you make that choice
To live life in the moment;
Sacrificially rejoice.
When your hair has fallen out -
It's no time for a perm.
I think it's time for pointing -
Pointing at the pachyderm.

You seek the everlasting arms
To shield you from the storm
And melt the piercing chill within
To once again be warm.
In the cold and fading darkness,
You cherish every therm.
I think it's time for pointing -
Pointing at the pachyderm.

Jacob's Well

In the fiercest heat of the day
A woman made her way;
Going for water, so they say.
She was heading for Jacob's Well.

As the well came into view,
A stranger sat there too.
He looked as though he knew
The history of Jacob's Well.

Before she'd time to think
He'd asked her for a drink;
Turned her face a shade of pink.
It happened at Jacob's Well.

She asked him "How can you,
A man – and especially a Jew,
Do what people just don't do
Even here at Jacob's Well?"

He said "If you knew God I think,
You would ask me for a drink
Of living water – you're on the brink.
Here today at Jacob's Well."

His next words took her aback
"Get your husband - come right back
Or are you losing track
Of your beaus at Jacob's Well?"

She agreed she was not wed
And the stranger shook his head.
Quiet were the words he said
In the shade of Jacob's Well.

"What you said is true.
Five husbands have had you
And now another man who's new
Is sending you to Jacob's Well."

She said "It is as plain as day –
A prophet has come to stay
But worship God – which way –
Jerusalem or Jacob's Well?"

He said "The time is now
When 'where' gives way to 'how'
And men's spirits need to bow
Round the world and Jacob's Well."

Other men came back with food
And, though they weren't exactly rude,
She should leave that's understood.
Only men at Jacob's Well.

She went rushing up and down
Saying "Guess what I've found.
Maybe Messiah's come to town
I met him at Jacob's Well."

(Don't You Remember) The Belvederes?

Pub trivia quiz last Thursday night.
Second last question; I got it right!
They were really quite big -
Especially round here;
Don't you remember the Belvederes?

The singer was tall; what was his name?
He never quite made the Hall of Fame.
Roman Candle splutters .
Then disappears.
Don't you remember the Belvederes?

Living legends now; if they're still alive;
Their greatest year was nineteen sixty-five.
Focus your memory
Until the mist clears.
Don't you remember the Belvederes?

I didn't invent them; at least I don't think.
In the story of rock - a missing link.
I'll form a tribute band
And roll back the years.
Don't you remember the Belvederes?

Even now it isn't too late for a legend to form.
They were never red hot but at least they're still warm.
You'll hear what I mean
If you open your ears.
Don't you remember the Belvederes?

Misunderstood except by the faithful fans who came;
Who if truth can be told were mainly known by name.
They greeted each song
With appreciative cheers.
Don't you remember the Belvederes?

There were the records; at least four on LP
And two of them now are out on CD.
As good as "Walsingham."
Longer than "Salisbury Gears."
Don't you remember the Belvederes?

Though decades have passed; it could be yesterday.
Unscramble the eggs, get back under way.
Turn back the clock
Redeem the lost years
Don't you remember the Belvederes?

Dead Man

How can you love a dead man?
I find that very odd.
Some distant, foreign joiner
Who was also Son of God?

How can you love this Jesus
When he isn't here to see?
It might have been so different
On windswept Galilee.

How can you love a stranger
Whom you have never met?
And yet you tell me somehow
He has paid, in full, your "debt".

How can you love a hero
Who died in the attempt?
Death claimed another victim.
He was not in fact exempt.

How can you love this man when
You already have a wife?
Is it a different kind of love
Or a different kind of life?

How can you love a teacher,
Who taught so many years ago,
That we should love our neighbour
And also love our foe?

How can you love a Jew from
The so-called Chosen Race?
It doesn't seem that likely.
Don't overstate the case.

How can you love a spirit
That you say's everywhere?
I'm sorry I can't see him
No matter how I stare.

How can you love a saviour
Who's saved you, please, from what?
Does it mean you'll never die?
You tell me it does not.

This song is full of questions
But the answers aren't here
I'll leave it open-ended
And anything but clear.

And if it makes you wonder
Then I'll be satisfied.
As they say, the truth is out there -
It's impossible to hide.

Adrenaline and Grace

Come now tell me, Christian;
Are you feeling very tired,
Bruised and world weary,
Distinctly uninspired?
No way you'd run with horses;
You'd rarely run with men,
Though you might go for a brisk walk
Every now and then.

If we would run with horses,
And take part in the race,
We need (not in that order)
Adrenaline and grace.

The prophet Jeremiah
Had an awful lot to say;
About almond branches, boiling pots
And the yielding potter's clay.
It wasn't all disaster;
He saw some awesome sights
And pointed to our constant need
To reach for higher heights.

Despair's our first reaction
When something thwarts our plan;
Forgetting that the ways of God
Are not the ways of man.
But if we persevere,
Then, when our race is run -
"You are my faithful servant
I am pleased with what you've done."

Stuck Inside of Drumcree
(with the Garvaghy Blues Again)

She can see him from her window in his uniform so cute.
If she was a sniper, he'd be so easy to shoot.
History repeats repeats and then repeats again,
Stuck inside of Drumcree with the Garvaghy blues again.

In a divided country, it's the lovers suffer most.
If you can feel his sorrow you're getting too damn close.
Accentuate the positive and forget about the pain,
Stuck inside of Drumcree with the Garvaghy blues again.

The television pundits think they've got it sussed.
Love will conquer hatred because they think it must.
The streets will bloom with flowers and hide the brutal stain,
Stuck inside of Drumcree with the Garvaghy blues again.

She remembers when they met - a summer day like this.
Their first date together, the undivisive kiss.
They've everything to lose and not a lot to gain,
Stuck inside of Drumcree with the Garvaghy blues again.

They lean towards despair; they rarely dare to hope.
They call it "realistic" - it's the only way to cope.
Is finding a solution beyond the human brain,
Stuck inside of Drumcree with the Garvaghy blues again?

Europa Hotel

I remember it well - the Europa Hotel.
We were at a bus stop in the rain.
I recalled all the scenes from the TV screens
Of the horror and carnage and pain.

And I thought could it be, we have finally got free
From the violently held points of view?
And has the hotel rebuilt somehow been instilled
With a facade that's actually true?

When I came to this town, I nearly fell down
To my knees to kiss the quayside.
This could have been mine in a different design;
And - who knows - it still might.

The rain still poured down on this grey, damaged town
And yet a welcome extended to me,
Though when we got on the bus I felt less nervous
At the thought of rerun history.

Back at the boat with a rain-sodden coat
And a timetable nearly not met.
I'll remember so well the Europa Hotel
It's never felt this good getting wet.

I Don't Do Flowers

Maybe it's my old hay fever.
It isn't the expense.
Maybe it is flowers'
Fleeting, fading transience.
I've written you a lot of poems
Shopped for gifts for hours.
Sorry it's the way I am
My love - I don't do flowers.

And anyway where's the flower
That could compare with you?
You're my very precious rose
I'm glad that God picked you.

You keep hoping for a bouquet -
Or at least a bunch -
Or maybe just a single stem
At some romantic lunch.
Trees I love and growing things
And leafy woodland bowers;
But plants look best just where they grow
My love - I don't do flowers.

This isn't just another song;
This song's completely true,
Saying what I want to say
Carole, I love you.
At your gentle inspiration
I use my writing powers;
This love has such diverse expression.
My love - I don't do flowers.

Fluffy Dice

They say a man is living
Somewhere near here in his car.
It hasn't got its wheels on
So it can't go very far.
It all sounds quite horrendous
And really far from nice.
We could brighten up his habitat
We could buy him fluffy dice.

We really should do something;
If we could just think what to do.
We're all so keen to act
There's already quite a queue.
We could ask him for a meal;
We might even do it twice.
At the end of the day
Are we just serving fluffy dice?

We really must do something;
He can't go on this way.
Call the social work department
Or a homeless charity.
We could help him fill in forms.
We could offer good advice;
But would it count for more
Than just giving fluffy dice?

We're not enthusiastic
'Cause we don't know where he's been.
The car's no sanitation
So he can't be very clean.
We can't expose our families
To the risk of nits or lice.
So that's why we're restricted
To a gift of fluffy dice.

If you'll arrange a flag day
We will gladly fill your can,
Expressing solidarity
With the brotherhood of man.
We'll buy the very best ones
And we won't remove the price.
They might be very costly
But they're still just fluffy dice.

Jesus said "Whatever
You do for the least of these,
You also do for me
And God your Father sees."
Are the victims of our charity
Even poorer than church mice;
And is our love just random
Like the roll of fluffy dice?

The Frail Broken Children of Dust

Is that a light at the end of the tunnel,
Or the night train heading my way?
The darkness is never quite total
Isn't that what they always say?
This is the time of despair
As disasters pile up like a soap.
I'm nearing the end of my tether
Reviewing the end of a rope.

Betrayal and insult and sorrow -
How bitter the wounds of a friend.
Sorrows are piling like snowdrifts;
Christmasless winter won't end.
Some days are blacker than others -
Walking by touch not by sight.
Is it true that the shadows get darker,
The closer you get to the light?

The phone's off the hook in the evening.
The letter box only eats junk.
There's veins on my wrist when I shave.
There's no bottles left to be drunk.
There's a whispering voice in the spirit;
Destruction is always at hand.
There's reluctance to face off the challenge
And opposing it then to stand.

The future is always uncertain
Except to the One who is there.
What's past is only the prologue
The real show is waiting up there.
These are the days of rebuilding,
Of consolation and starting to trust.
Learning the wonderful destiny
Of the frail broken children of dust.

John Prine Derivative New Home Moving Blues

Woke up this morning; it's our last day in this place.
I swore I saw my sadness mirrored in your face.
This has been a good house - I'll be sad to leave behind.
Forget it honey - it's too late to change your mind.

We've got the John Prine derivative
New home moving blues.

Everything is packed and the van gets here at ten.
There's still lots to do in the time from now till then.
Gaze through each window for one last wistful time.
Try to frame the memories; try to set them down in rhyme.

I'm not looking forward to finding things in the right box.
Favourite old key rings; new keys for different locks.
A brand new uniform for a brand new school.
Rooms that shrink when they're away from the surveyor's rule.

Life is full of changes, life is full of moving on.
We're pilgrims in this world and possibly beyond.
I'm too old for this; I cannot stand the pace.
I'll only move if I stay near your smiling face.

The Year of Jubilee

The Spirit of the Lord has come; He has anointed me
To tell the good news to the poor
And tell the prisoners they are free.
The blind again shall have their sight; injustice shall not be
This is the year the Lord has made;
The year of Jubilee.

Jesus broke the prison walls; He Himself the Way.
He did it two thousand years ago
And still does it today.
What He did in the Bible, He can do for you and me.
This is the year the Lord has made;
The year of Jubilee.

There are many types of prison, far from the light of day.
If you want to live outside
There only is one way.
Jesus alone has got the power; He can set you free
This is the year the Lord has made;
The year of Jubilee.

Stone walls do not a prison make nor iron bars a jail.
Unless the Lord has set you free,
Your freedom dream will fail.
Don't say there is no answer and we're stuck with what must be.
This is the year the Lord has made;
The year of Jubilee.

Judge Puffenberger

Judge Puffenberger, will you take a message, please.
Write it down most carefully so the words you use are these;
Tell the happy couple upon this special day;
We are thinking of them though we're many miles away.

Judge Puffenberger, can you please make it clear
That we are thinking of them with best wishes most sincere.
Tell the happy couple "May God bless both of you";
Our friend, Eleanor, and our new friend, Donald, too.

Judge Puffenberger, can you tell us all is well
Both with Mr Donald and Mrs Ellie Avanelle.
The name will come with practice; the love likewise will grow.
Time can make it stronger; listen, please - we know.

Judge Puffenberger, if you think you know her face;
She's walked this way before, been married in this place.
Let's hope this is the real one - a love that will not end.
That they will be together as lover, mate and friend.

Judge Puffenberger, we know it's late to call.
But it's surely better late than never not at all.
We'll maybe call you after to catch up with your day.
Remember that we're thinking, though we're many miles away.

Going to the Lebanon

With the prayers of all of us
In faith they soon will go.
Responding to the Master's call
To let all the people know.
May those who meet them understand
The reason why they came
On a gospel enterprise
Going in Your name.

Going to the Lebanon;
Father guard them well.
Keep them safe and make them bold -
The truth to tell.

On the pathway of Faith -
No way on holiday.
Going out to serve Him
As children of the Way.
May all the church keep praying
For their safe return.
For all that they will teach -
All that they will learn.

No one is an island
Or so the poet wrote.
We could lift the drawbridge
And then fill up the moat;
But that is not an option,
There's a world that needs to hear.
Let us discard our comfort
And trust to face our fear.

Magdalene Falls

There's a new man in her life it seems;
She's acting different now.
A great change has come over her;
We don't know why or how.
Now our Miss Horizontal
Is back upon her feet.
She's found a new profession;
She's left behind the street.

Magdalene falls
That's the way it seems
Has the city sinner
Found the man of her dreams?

She's moved to acts of kindness
From acts I won't describe.
A much more caring person
Than any Pharisee or scribe.
A total transformation;
It really is most strange,
And none of us have sussed yet
The reason for the change.

When first she met the preacher,
We all feared for the worse.
If she had seduced him,
He would not have been the first;
But in truth it isn't like that
Their love's a different kind.
It seems he understands her;
His love for her's not blind.

We'd like to go and ask her
What made her turn away
From her life of sullen whoring
To looking forward to each day;
But she's not the kind of person
With whom we socialise.
I think maybe the preacher
Sees her with different eyes.

To hear her talk about him
You'd think she was in love.
But she says "I am forgiven
And that's more than enough"

Noah's Got the Blues Again

Noah goes off by himself to a lonely place to cry.
He sits there in a bundle staring at the sky.
The remnants of the race where only eight remain.
The night is getting cloudy; could the deluge start again?

Noah's got the blues again;
But the rainbow is more broad.
There's every shade of colour
In the pure white light of God.

He still hears the anguished cries - panic, terror, fear;
As valleys, plains and mountains in turn all disappear.
The safety of his family was a consolation prize
As they sailed into the future beneath brooding sodden skies.

He tries to think it through; for his family have been blessed
But what about his neighbours, friends,
distant family and all the rest?
He cannot comprehend it; his understanding is so flawed.
Such a mystery - the fierce holiness of God.

And then he sees the rainbow, fragile colour in the sky,
And he slowly learns to hope; though he isn't quite sure why.
The symbol of the promise - judgement will not be so broad -
And always an escape route for those who trust in God.

No Pain Like His

There was no pain like His
Upon the brutal cross.
Convicted criminal
Who'd not broken any laws.

The scourge's acid bite
The jagged regal thorn.
Uncomplaining victim
Of the soldiers' sneering scorn.

The spear deep in His side.
The nails that pierced and tore.
Love amazing limitless;
How can anyone ignore?

The Father turned away;
The noon sky black as night.
The only fit atonement
To make the wrong things right.

There was no pain like His,
The pain that should be mine.
These words are stumbling, clumsy -
The love perfect, divine.

Outrage

Sulphur rains on Sodom
And we sit smugly by.
Our own goodness has saved us
It's those sinners time to die!
Homophobic fever
Has got the church in thrall;
If God destroyed all sinners
There'd be no-one left at all.

It's an outrage
An outrage - that is all.

A bomb blast in the city
There's a sickness in the land.
Whatever kind of diseased mind
Could this outrage have planned?
We crouch on moral high ground
Saying "see how low they stoop"
And draw a crumb of comfort
We're not yet a target group.

Let's weep with those who weep
And mourn with those who mourn.
Not just with the married
Or those who sleep alone.
Let's not react in judgement
But work at charity;
Trust that there's some meaning
In this monstrosity.

Shadow of Death

As we came back to the town, and left behind the park,
The sun was going down - it would very soon be dark.
West of us the tomb, bizarre against the sky;
Reminding us of - whom? Reminding us we would die.

We were walking in the shadow of death,
Shadow of death,
We were walking in the shadow of death.

It had been a lovely day; we hoped for many more.
Another happy memory; I've completely lost the score.
No point in keeping track, pushed forward by our hunger.
The aching from my back says "You're not getting any younger".

We were walking in the shadow of death,
Shadow of death,
We were walking in the shadow of death.

My living Christian faith transforms the thought of death;
Dispels the ghostly wraith breathing that final breath.
I don't want to die for ages - there's so much still to do.
Words to put on pages and ways of loving you.

We were dancing in the light of the sun,
Light of the sun.
We were dancing in the light of the sun.

She Tempted Me (Blues for Bathsheba)

It's very hard to justify
The fact I caused a man to die.
I was weak - a man of dust
Driven by a fevered lust;
But the fault was not all mine,
I was drunk with beauty not with wine.
I think that it was plain to see - she tempted me

Like a tiger that I could not tame
I saw her bathing without shame.
I could only in torment gaze
And plot and hope and count the days.
I could not escape, though I did try
And then sent her husband off to die.
In mitigation hear my plea - she tempted me.

A prophet acted out my sin
In ignorance I agreed with him.
Until he said I was the man;
That was the day the dreams began.
I know I took what wasn't mine,
But I am king - I can't resign.
I must fulfil my destiny - she tempted me.

Yet through our love there was a son;
And we have called him Solomon.
We believe that in God's plan
He will grow up a special man.
It doesn't mean we weren't wrong
It doesn't end this weeping song.
Mine the fault, though please agree - she tempted me.

The Love That Bleeds

At Easter we remember the greatest of God's deeds
Coming to our rescue - the love that bleeds.
Commandments condemn; sacrifice succeeds
Paid the price of freedom - the love that bleeds.

Oh my Lord – how great Your Love to die this way for me.
Amazed, I stand where Wesley stood, saying "And can it be?"
Lord, you satisfy my soul; You answer all my needs.
The greatest love the world will know - the love that bleeds.

The light shines brighter - darkness recedes.
On that green hill - the love that bleeds.
Your broken flesh the whole world feeds.
Amazing grace - the love that bleeds.

Living truth, not formal creeds.
Salvation winning - the love that bleeds.
Faith grows from mustard seeds,
Nourished by - the love that bleeds.

Full grown wheat or worthless weeds?
The difference is the love that bleeds.
Wise the man that message heeds.
Forgiving death - the love that bleeds.

Christmastime is Coming

Christmastime is coming and the shops are full of crap.
There's Santas by the dozen and there's reindeer milk on tap.
In every shopping centre the same CD is played;
Jona Lewie's "Cavalry" and the Christmas one by Slade.

Christmastime is coming and the shops are full of junk.
Tills are overheating and going "ching" and "plunk."
Look closely at the offers; I'm sure that you'll agree;
No matter what they're giving, be sure it isn't free.

Christmastime is coming and the shops are full of crud.
Cards drop through the door and Christmas parcels thud.
"Gimme, gimme, gimme" is the children's shout;
If they believe in Santa - or if they've sussed him out.

Christmastime is coming and some lives are full of pain.
Lonely people missing people they'll not see again.
Families end up fighting - every year's the same.
Stagger from the house and wonder why they came.

Christmastime is coming and the streets are full of slush.
The snow was picturesque but got trampled in the rush.
Wise men, shepherds, angels - are they just extras on a card?
I wish I could believe it but it's really very hard.

Christmastime is coming and the churches aren't full,
Except maybe the Watchnight, the exception to the rule.
What about the wise men coming from the east?
They tip the wink to Herod and his death squads are released.

Christmastime is coming; I wish that it was not.
I think there's something missing - although I don't know what.
Christmastime is coming, but I really can't see why
This commemorates a God who came to wash our feet - and die.

What about the stable; a king without a roof.
Not a God out there - distant, remote, aloof.
You say He came to join us - to share our joy and grief
And died upon a cross - on either side a thief.

Could He be the Saviour? And could it somehow be
That this tacky Christmas card contains good news for me?
It really is a puzzle - explain it now, please do.
It sounds like a fairy story - could it possibly be true?

Spirit Is Willing

We're weeping Lord for those who aren't here.
They know not what they're missing; we need to make that clear.
You're working, Lord, our hearts are not so hard;
And yet we still resist you; parts of our lives are barred.

We're turning, Lord, from the leaden ties that bind;
Finding a new freedom, we're prisoners unconfined.
You're doing that Lord; let us know your power -
Every minute of every day, not just the Sunday happy hour

We're praising Lord, songs that let us speak
Of how you are so wonderful and we're so cold and weak.
You're burning Lord; ignite our love and zeal.
Change the way we live and not just the way we feel.

We're trusting Lord, trusting You to act.
You only are the future - there is no turning back.
You're leading Lord - and we will follow You.
The ancient one of days - yet making all things new.

As We Baptise
(tune "In Praise of Islay")

On this day we gather here,
Family friends from far and near;
Let our praise ring true and clear
As we baptise this infant.

Lord draw close this special day.
Bless this family now we pray.
Guide them safely on their way.
As we baptise this baby.

Thank the Father, Sprit, Son
For new life not long begun.
Lord this day Your will be done
As we baptise this young girl/boy.

What we do is in Your will.
Let us feel that holy thrill.
With Your Spirit now us fill.
As we baptise her/him now.

What She Could
(tune "The Water is Wide")

Alabaster box of precious nard,
Costing the wages for one whole year.
She broke the box and spread the scent
Anointing Him while He was near.

And what she did was what she could
Not scared off by what folk might say;
Held nothing back but gave her all -
A lesson still for us today.

We try so hard to earn God's love;
When all the time it is freely gi'en;
Because the ways of fallen man
Are not the ways of God in heaven.

Let what we do be what we can,
Responding to His gracious love.
We can't give more than all we are.
We can't give less - that's not enough.

Calypso Hosanna
(tune "Calypso Carol")

On the road into Jerusalem,
A crowd had gathered and, in front of them,
Rode a king without a diadem;
A lowly donkey was His steed.

Sing hosanna sing out joyfully
Because the Lord has set us free
When He died that death so willingly
So that we can be free indeed!

On the road there were palm branches spread,
Showing truth was what the prophets said.
Five days later though He would be dead;
Not that darkness would succeed.

On the road that led to Calvary
To pay sin's price that day for you and me;
The only perfect sacrifice was He -
God sent the answer to our need.

On our road now He will walk beside,
Our living saviour, our friend and our guide.
We the church shall one day be his bride.
Till then follow. Let Him lead.

Harvest Hymn
(tune "We plough the fields and scatter")

We gather round the produce
the flowers and the food,
And, pausing for a moment,
reflect with gratitude.
How gracious are You Father.
We know that it is true;
The measure of our love is this -
how much we give to You.

Sing a song of harvest,
A harvest song of praise.
We thank You Lord, Yes thank You Lord
So good in all Your ways.

The sowing and the harvest,
the seasons' rise and fall,
The majesty of nature
and You have made it all.
We take so much for granted
and treat it as our right.
We really should know better
as children of the light.

This world is ill-divided
and we must share the blame.
We need to work for justice
and do it in Your Name.
This world is well provided
to serve each person's need.
The balance is distorted
by selfishness and greed.

Coming Home

I'm not talking 'bout your motherland,
I'm talking 'bout your Father God;
For He alone is your home sweet home
Though you have been abroad.
Coming home like the prodigal
Towards his Father's place.
Returned from sin and was welcomed in
By His Father's smiling face.

This is the year of coming home,
Though you have been away.
This is the year of coming home,
Of coming home to stay.
This is the year of coming home
This is the year of grace.
This is the year of coming home
To our Father's smiling face.

I'm not talking 'bout a nation state,
I'm talking 'bout the Kingdom come.
Of His rule on Earth and the second birth
Into the Lordship of God's Son.
Coming home, never more to leave,
Trying to live the way He says.
We need not fear for we're welcomed here
By our Father's smiling face.

New Songs
(tune "Thy Hand O God Has Guided")

New songs are still being written to praise our living Lord;
Some based upon our feelings - more based upon Your Word;
But this the common factor, which always should shine through,
With hymns ancient and modern, we still shall sing to You.

Though styles of music vary, You still remain the same;
But what is all important, we praise Your holy name.
With words our parents cherished or words newspaper new,
If, in the truth we worship, we still shall sing to You.

Without Your Holy Spirit our singing is just songs.
With unity and service our praise to You belongs.
Alpha through to omega; ageless yet ever new;
With hymns ancient and modern, we still shall sing to You.

Each rising generation must seek You for their own,
For You have no grandchildren; each child is Yours alone.
The Church is never shrinking, since Pentecost it grew;
And on through endless ages we still shall sing to You.

The Wounds Are Still There

The wounds He bore so willingly,
The wounds He bore to set me free,
The wounds He bore on Calvary;
The wounds are still there.

As Thomas did in that locked room,
When he saw love ris'n from the tomb,
He knelt and honoured Jesus whom
Was his Lord and his God.

The wounds upon hands, feet and side,
The wounds that Heaven opened wide.
The wounds of love being crucified;
The wounds are still there.

I needn't put my finger there,
The gape of love and endless care.
The greatest love that ever dared
Was my Lord and my God

The wounds of chosen willing pain.
The wounds of loss for greater gain.
The wounds eternally remain;
The wounds are still there.

One day all of the world will see,
Acknowledging on bended knee,
Reluctantly or joyfully;
He's our Lord and our God.

Joy
(tune "Ode to Joy")

Lord, the praises that we bring You,
On this brand new Sabbath day,
Are the foretaste of the praises
Which will ring eternally;
For in Heaven praise will continue
Ever onwards with no end;
Praises to the living Jesus
Saviour, Master, Lord and Friend.

Words are not enough to hold
The overflow of grateful hearts;
Yet our praise can be restricted;
Celebrate in fits and starts.
Give us joy without conditions,
Joy that praises You all day,
Joy that comes from You, Joy-giver,
Joy that never goes away.

For the love that You have shown us
What response is good enough;
But to praise You come whatever
And tell others of That love?
Lord, the praises that we bring You,
On this blessed Sabbath day,
Are the foretaste of the praises
Which will ring eternally.

In the Kingdom
(tune "The Work of the Weavers")
("The Welly Boot Song")

"Many a mickle maks a muckle" - that's what granny said;
It's lingered in my memory. It's rattling in my head.
I'd like to weave it in a song to illustrate this thread;
For that's how it is in the kingdom.

In the kingdom last is first and first is last.
A tiny seed can grow into something that is vast.
Jesus' words they will go on
though heaven and earth are past.
For that's how it is in the kingdom.

A rich man at the offering with his thick wad of notes
And a wee widow woman in her shabby hat and coat;
And yet it was of her gift that Jesus said "take note";
For that's how it is in the kingdom.

If you have a seed of faith - it matters not how small,
You can say to a mountain - it matters not how tall,
You tell it "be uplifted" and it in the sea will fall;
For that's how it is in the kingdom.

At this time of year of Advent, which we are marking now,
God became a man and the Bible tells us how.
The king of kings - a tiny babe in the manger of a cow;
For that's how it is in the kingdom.

Fruit Trees
(tune "Rowan Tree")

Like fruit trees which in orchards grow,
And do by His design,
We share with them a purpose clear
To bear rich fruit divine.
For if God's Spirit lives in us,
We should abundant be,
Producing fruit to quench a world
That's gasping thirstily.
Let us bear fruit.

Such fruit as love and joy and peace
And patience learned from You.
From servant hearts let kindness act
And lives of goodness too.
Faithful gentle self controlled;
Let us display all nine.
Our Father is the gardener.
Our Saviour is the vine.
Let us bear fruit.

Apart from Him we have no sap,
Our branches dry and bare;
And yet if we be grafted in
His life we'll truly share.
He will increase our fruitfulness,
Our branches He will trim,
And we shall bear the sweetest fruit
If we remain in Him.
Let us bear fruit.

Centenary Hymn
(tune "Sine Nomine")

One hundred years of service in this place;
Of seeking the Lord and living in His Grace.
The times they have changed, as change they always must.
Come now let us praise Him in whom alone we trust.

One hundred years of laughter and of tears.
The sharing of lives - the joys, the hopes, the fears.
Come Spirit of God and bind us into one.
Come now let us praise Him; let us praise the Holy One.

One hundred years and thousands went before.
Some sacrificed their lives and fell in war.
We shall not forget the saints who paved the way.
Come now let us praise Him for He is alive today.

One hundred years of serving those around;
Of sharing His Love and telling what we've found.
May all that we do display the truth we bring.
Come now let us praise Him; let us praise our servant King.

One hundred years; God holds how many more.
We don't know the future; we know Who it's for.
The living Lord Jesus - Saviour and our friend.
Come now let us praise Him - our beginning and our end.

If Christ Be Not Raised Up
(tune "To God be the Glory")

If Christ be not raised up our faith is in vain
And death is victorious – we'll not live again.
Our faith just a crutch upon which we now lean
By trusting in something that has not been seen.

Jesus lives! Jesus lives! By the power of God
Jesus lives! Jesus lives! Let us spread it abroad
Death has been dismantled – He's taken its sting
Give praise now to Jesus our true risen king!

Our faith is not futile if we trust in Him.
Jesus by His dying has dealt with our sin.
Our faith is fulfilled for He rose up again
And with us forever our Lord will remain.

By His resurrection He proved all He said.
He died in our place and then rose from the dead.
Our lives should bear witness in all that we do;
Our Lord is alive and the Good News is true.

We Can Count on You

One for the one true God who rules over earth and sky;
Two for the Testaments that tell us the reason why;
Three for the three in one - the Holy Trinity;
Four for the Gospel books which tell what You did for me.

Unnumbered blessings,
Showered on me, showered on you;
Father, we know the truth,
We can count on You,
Yes, Abba, we can count on You,
Yes, Papa, we can count on You.

Five for the Pentateuch and the five-fold ministry;
Six for creation's days in which You made humanity;
Seven for completeness - the Sabbath day of rest;
Eight for a new beginning in which we can all be blessed.

Nine for the Spirit's gifts and also when the Spirit came;
Ten for the Ten Commandments, honouring Your holy name;
Eleven for the eleven disciples who stood while Judas fell;
Twelve for the Hebrew Tribes - the Children of Israel.

Been There, Done That, Worn the Crown of Thorns

Didn't grasp the majesty,
Laid all of that aside.
Came to earth to die for us
And on a donkey ride.
Revealing God and washing feet,
The high King lowly born.
Been there, done that, worn the crown of thorns.

Streaks of spit dried on His face;
Palette with the blood.
How sharp the sound of splitting skin
And the hammer's sullen thud.
There was no beauty left in Him;
His body bruised and torn.
Been there, done that, worn the crown of thorns.

Two thieves in that place of death
Each acted differently;
One poured out invective,
One said "Remember me."
One was saved – do not despair;
One was lost – be warned.
Been there, done that, worn the crown of thorns.

There's nowhere we can go in life;
No heartache we can bear,
That He hasn't sampled
And taken the lion's share.
Been to hell and back again,
Returned that Easter morn.
Been there, done that, worn the crown of thorns.

Main Street

If Jesus walked down Main Street,
Would he hang His head and weep
At the empty aimless lives of shepherdless sheep?

If Jesus walked down Main Street,
Would the hungry still be fed;
Not just with loaves and fishes but with the living bread?

If Jesus walked down Main Street,
Would the prisoners be released?
Would the crowds come flocking
To the great King's wedding feast?

For as many as would receive Him, Jesus died to save them all.
From Jerusalem to Main Street; will you heed the Saviour's call?

If Jesus walked down Main Street, would He still face ridicule?
Would He be followed by the outcasts - a festival of fools?

If Jesus walked down Main Street,
Would two thousand years erase
The holes in hands and feet and thorn scars on His face?

Wounds healed but gaping, still visible above.
Wounds He bore for Main Street; that amazing gift of love.

If Jesus walked down Main Street
Would doors open to His knock?
Or would the bolts be thrown back and keys turned in the lock?

If Jesus walked down Main Street and came into this hall;
Would we choose to fully follow - forsaking all?

Without Siobhan

He can't enjoy the present
He can't enjoy the past.
He can't look forward to the future
He knows that all things pass.
There is a nagging question
Does he want to carry on?
Does life still have any meaning without Siobhan?

There's a harshness in the moonlight,
There's a coldness in the sun.
The old pleasures don't engage him
But he can't tell anyone.
Joy has turned to ashes;
All that's good is gone.
The only taste is bitter without Siobhan.

His friends all want to reach him
To let him know they care.
How can they feel his sorrow;
How can they be there?
The hopes, the dreams, the planning
Out of time still-born;
And now there is bleak nothing without Siobhan.

Yet there will be a better day
But no-one can tell him that.
His blinds are tightly closed
No chink peeps through a slat;
But hope's around the corner -
There will be a brighter dawn,
But flecked with stabs of sorrow without Siobhan.

Working Granny

I think my granny's working, but they won't say what she does.
Every time I try to ask, they say "Don't make a fuss".
I don't think she's a teacher; I don't think she's a nurse.
I don't think she's a tax inspector. I think it's something worse.

She must be on the late shift - she only works at night;
And mainly at the weekend - says she never sees the light.
She's a really lovely granny; she buys us lots of toys.
It's not that she has favourites;
but she likes girls more than boys.

I've never met my grandpa; don't even know his name.
He might have been a sportsman; she met him at the game.
I'd have liked to know him; he might have been a lot of fun.
They say there is no telling - he could have been anyone.

I don't think she'll be retiring; doesn't have a pension plan.
She might be a chef - they said something
about mutton dressed as lamb.
She dozes when she comes here; she's tired although they say
"How can she be sleepy - she's not been on her feet all day?"

Her bag is full of sweeties and things called condoms too.
No matter how much I ask they won't tell me what they do.
The only time I asked her was the time I saw her cry.
She said they're her medicine - without them she might die.

Paint Yer Bollards

You can paint your kerbstones
With multi-coloured hue.
Where I stay the streets are grey -
With a hint of doggy-doo.

What a pretty picture;
What a sorry mess;
Repeat again the wars of then
In semi-modern dress.

You can paint yer bollards
Red and white and blue;
So we know which way you go
When you express your point of view.

You can paint your bollards
Orange and white and green.
You fly your flag - a tattered rag
And it somehow seems obscene.

You can wear your colours
In a big parade.
Robotic march that's stiff as starch;
Where nothing new is said.

You can go not far away
To hear a different song;
Where colours change, souls rearrange
And I feel that I belong.

Living Black and White

I had in mind to say life is generally grey -
It's very rarely clear cut black and white;
But I had another think before I set this down in ink
About the border line dividing wrong and right.

Most of the time we know the road where we should go
And debating points are simply an excuse.
We like to slip the reins because we're weak and vain
And we like the thought of one day breaking loose.

Black and white, black and white.
Wrong is wrong and right is right.
We are children of the light;
Let us spend our lives in living black and white.

There is a guiding light even in the darkest night
And we are never ever truly on our own.
There's a most compelling guide who speaks to us inside
And sees us even when we're alone.

The edge we choose to blur, and we hope our friends concur,
Because they're tempted as we are.
We follow how we feel though that is fleeting, scarcely real.
Like foolish men and unimagined star.

Make us strong and brave and no longer the slaves
Of life-hating things that scuttle in the night.
And give us grace to be the joyful ones set free -
Shining ones in living black and white.

Horoscope Blues

I woke up this morning and I read my horoscope.
It said "you'll have a good day" and so I got up with hope.
I went down to breakfast and I made a cup of tea.
The leaves were very promising - I was happy as can be.
So I've no need to worry for every sign is good
But I'll be on the safe side and I'll take a knock on wood.

No! No! No-one knows the future.
No! No! No-one but the Lord knows.
Beware!
The Devil tries to trick you.
Follow God's plan for you
One day at a time.

I went to get my palm read by a gypsy in a tent.
Her words were reassuring but I wonder what they meant.
She also warned of accidents so I left her with less hope
And fifteen seconds later I tripped over the tent rope.
People try to sneer at it. They say it makes no sense
Can gypsies with their crystal balls really read the future tense?

Many times in history, man has tried to read the signs;
Consulted chicken entrails and cabalistic lines;
And so been drawn to evil and the Devil has the laugh
At the increased wastage of wheat among the chaff.
The Devil's such a vicious foe that no-one dare relax;
He's expert at camouflage and covering his tracks.

Days Gone By

I woke up one morning and I was middle-aged.
My life felt like the third act of a dull play being staged.
Older than Dylan Thomas raging at the fading light;
Older than Wolfgang Amadeus when he went into the night.
Thinking back the question's "when" not "why" -
I'm weeping for the days gone by.

I'm weeping for the good things more than for the bad.
Is that a warning sign that I'm starting to go mad?
Not looking back in anger - I'm looking back in grief
At the massive haul of some sinister time thief.
I'm further from my day of birth than from the day I'll die -
I'm weeping for the days gone by.

Ageing doesn't faze me; I'm at comfort with myself;
But, when something stirs up memories
from some forgotten dusty shelf,
I feel an ache of emptiness that I struggle to explain.
I would not drink elixirs to seize my youth again.
I won't try to act younger - no hair colour I'll apply -
I'm weeping for the days gone by.

The Bible talks about locust years; how I long to have them back;
Wilderness years nowhere near the narrow track.
By grace not by my efforts - no matter how hard I try -
It doesn't stop me weeping - weeping for the days gone by.

The Victor

To the eye without the faith light,
Life is full of cruel jokes;
Where spanners lurk round corners;
Just waiting for your spokes.
Sometimes when one door closes
The next slams in your face;
And that would be the sum of it,
Without amazing grace.

Though you might lose the battle,
You've already won the war.
Stand up in the victory
Of the one you're fighting for!

A long and weary journey,
Which you might think will never end;
But you will receive a welcome
From your greatest ever friend.
Then you will know no sorrow;
Then you will know no pain.
So let me now repeat it
And sing out once again;

This is a time of wordless dread,
The valley's full of fear.
The dreadful day
Is drawing ever more near;
And there seems nothing you can do
Except trust this is the Way;
For you have got a greater hope
And you can now say;

On a hilltop called Golgotha
Your destiny was sealed,
When the one who made all things
To death his life did yield.
It seemed all hope was over,
But then on the third day -
He burst out from the grave again
Which is why I now can say;

And those you leave behind you
Will know such painful times
Though maybe they'll be comforted
By remembering these rhymes;
For you will be reunited
On the resurrection day
And all can join the chorus
And now with me can say;

*Though you might lose the battle
You've already won the war.
Stand up in the victory
Of the one who won the war!*

Call God

You can call God your Father.
You can call God your light.
You can call God the only thing
That gets you through the night.
You can call God "ground of being."
You can call God Paraclete.
You can call God filthy names
And shock them in the street.

But call God, call God,
Call on His name.
In this life where towers crumble
He always is the same.

You can call God whenever.
You can call in deep despair.
You can call God although
You don't believe that He is there.
You can call God next Thursday.
You can call God today.
You can call God in the knowledge
He knows what you will say.

You can call God in words.
You can simply weep and groan.
You can call God in the darkness
When you feel the most alone.
~~You can call God anything.~~
You can call God what you feel.
You can call God in confidence;
He wants you to be real.

But call God, call God -
His line's never engaged.
He listens to the broken,
The hurting, the enraged.

But call God, call God,
Call on His name.
In this life where towers crumble
He always is the same.

Across the Decades

He flew across the Channel
One hundred years ago.
They say he was a Frenchman
By the name of Bleriot.
My daughter flew it recently;
I was so sad to see her go.
One more change
It's constant change;
Can I take any more?

Across the decades
So many things have changed.
One thing though is constant;
Jesus is the same.

The good old "Waverley"
Was built upon the Clyde;
Replacement for one sunk in war
Coming from the Dunkirk side.
My father was the designer -
To me a source of pride.
Times rush by
And fathers die
And children's hearts are sore.

Thirty miles of tunnel
Opened fifteen years ago.
It's called the Channel Tunnel -
As if you didn't know.
Waters billow deep above,
While trains roll through below.
A long held dream
An epic scheme;
There are so many more.

We have crossed that Channel
By tunnel, boat and plane;
But upon a cross of wood
The king of life was slain.
Heaven and earth will pass away
But His words will remain.
He came to us;
He died for us;
Now He lives for evermore.

O Little Town of Bethlehem 2

O little town of Bethlehem,
Your streets now run with blood.
Instead of throngs of angel songs,
The tank shells sear and thud.
Sporadic sound of gunfire;
The threat of sudden death.
The hopes and fears of all the years
On tiptoe hold their breath.

O little town of Bethlehem,
This world has lost its way;
Ignoring the message
Revealed on Christmas Day.
Politics and religion,
Another cause to hate.
Angels above remember love -
But the town will have to wait.

O little town of Bethlehem,
Your past is like a dream.
With little hope to help us cope,
The future blacker seems.
Yet in your holy history,
So many years gone by,
The Price of Peace, star in the East,
Gives a hope that will not die.

O little town of Bethlehem,
When will the violence end?
When man to man holds out his hand
To brother and to friend?
There is a source of perfect love,
This world can never give;
Born in you and died for you
And will forever live.

Caring

Won't you let me bear your load
For at least a little while
As we travel on this road together -
Beyond the second mile?
Love is action not a feeling.
Love is where we live.
Love our deepest fears revealing.
Love helps us forgive.

We're caring - for one another.
We're sharing - sister, brother.
We're daring - to accept each other.
Let the cleansing love of Jesus
Infect our daily lives.

Won't you let me feel your sorrow
As tears roll down my face?
A brighter day may dawn tomorrow
Lightened by His grace.
Love is truth and not pretending.
Love is who we are.
Love is a road never ending;
Love never says "too far".

We're caring - for one another.
We're sharing - sister, brother.
We're daring - to accept each other
Let the healing love of Jesus
Restore our daily lives.

The Routes of Coincidence

Wheels will turn
And fires will burn.
I will leave
But I return to you.

I don't know
Which way to go
But I find out
Soon - I'm not slow to you.

I can't see waves on the sea
But they bear
Homecoming me to you.

Midnight creep.
The hills are steep -
I'd climb them all to bring
My sleep to you.

Birds grow still
And tigers will
Explain the sense;
The hunters thrill to you.

Routes of coincidence
I cannot understand
All I need is confidence
To follow your command.

Burning Bridges

Hurry on through a one-way world
Till you find somewhere nice to stay.
It will exist in your future -
You can forget yesterday.

Look at all my burning bridges
As I leave that life behind.
The past is best forgotten
Uncramp the future in your mind.

Don't look for easy answers.
Don't think life will always make sense.
Sometimes here and now it lets you down
And the past just makes you tense.

Look at all my burning bridges -
The cord has been severed now.
All I see is gold old brand new.
It'll soon grow old again one day.

Looks like you on the other side;
You're the only thing I'll miss.
I had to leave - you know I did.
I'm sorry that it came to this.

Look at all my burning bridges
That will never more be crossed.
Onwards is an easy choice
Now that the only retreat is lost.

Past and Future Echo

Don't be too explicit,
Someone might believe you.
Leave it more implicit,
Lest someone deceive you.
Keep it as a secret
That only we two know.
Keep it as a secret
Until the seed can grow.

Was it only last week
That I heard you say
"It's underneath the surface
But rising every day"?
There's no way that we can
Know what the future's bringing;
But I can hear the echo
Of subliminal singing.

Past and future echo
In and all around you.
Past and future echo
Forever older, newer.
Underneath the surface,
Deep inside your mind;
If we start to burrow
Who knows what we'll find.

Pinstripe Gypsy

I get up each morning
And I put on my suit.
I think it's silly
But my mum thinks it's cute.
Then I go to the office
From where I'm sent out
Because in my job I must travel about.
I'm a pinstripe gypsy;
I must travel about.

I get to the client
And they give me a room;
But it's not mine,
I must give it back soon.
I wish I could stay
For I like it out here
But I've got to move on
'Cause my charge-out's too dear.
I'm a pinstripe gypsy;
My charge-out's too dear.

The office staff people
Are friendly to me;
They give me a biscuit
And a nice cup of tea;
But they all wonder
Why the job is like this.
Alack and alas
That's how hard it is.
I'm a pinstripe gypsy
How hard it is.

We travel by train,
By car or by bus.
The office arranges
To cut down the fuss.
Not bloodhound or watchdog
Far less a sentry.
I am a guardian angel
Of double entry.
I'm a pinstripe gypsy
Maintain double entry.

I get home each evening
And I take off my suit.
I put on my jeans
And relax in my boots.
I sit by the fire
And I watch my TV.
Another day gone
Is there no hope for me?
I'm a pinstripe gypsy;
Is there no hope for me?

Chameleons

Underneath the moon
We softly sang in tune.
Underneath the sun
We had a lot of fun.
Underneath the cloud
We escaped the crowd.
Underneath the blue sky
We each had you and I.

Chameleons. Chameleons
Creatures of the place,
Changing for convenience
Not for each other.

Sitting in that bar
My mind it wandered far
On its nightly prowl
A wolf without a howl.

Pierced

My soul was pierced - as by a sword -
By what they did to my son, my Lord.
Unflinching love rebuffed with hate
And I stood there to weep and wait.

My soul was pierced - as by a spear -
With helpless love I suffered near
In a knot of grief and bitter pain
For the boy that I'd not see again.

My soul was pierced - as by a knife -
As his broken body bled his life;
Naked and helpless like day one
When I first held close my new born son.

Long ago an old man said my soul would pierc-ed be
As he praised God for my son and gave a prophecy
That tied in with the wonder words
The angel spoke to me
When he brought the awesome news
Of my chosen pregnancy.

My soul was pierced - as by a blade -
When in borrowed grave my child was laid;
Like his cuckoo birth in that manger bare
Except there was no hatred there.

My soul was pierced - as if by ice -
At this strange and brutal sacrifice.
The pain too great to comprehend
That this was not the bitter end.

It Should've Been Me

It could've been me,
It should've been me,
Nailed to that cross of wood;
But they set me free,
Took him for me;
As in my place he stood.

From a rebel band,
Condemned to stand
At Pilate's judgement seat.
Rebellion failed,
A prisoner jailed
To face the great defeat.

Barabbas name
Brought family shame,
But it means "the father's son."
Distinctly odd -
For "Son of God"
Some called the other one.

It could've been me,
It should've been me,
Upon Golgotha Hill;
But he went for me
To Calvary;
I can't believe it still.

Plucked like fruit,
A substitute,
Took my crime and death and pain;
Willingly -
It looked to me -
To let me live again.

It could've been me,
It should've been me,
A rebel only fit to die.
Now where to go?
I need to know
Who it was that died and why.

Leaving "I Love You"

Sometimes words get in the way
Of saying what we want to say,
Until we strip the wood away,
Leaving "I love you."

The shy young lover tries to speak
His words don't flow, instead they leak.
And, like his knees, turn strangely weak,
Leaving "I love you."

The song creaks with theology,
Confessing faith intellectually;
But is the heart there beating free,
Saying "I love you?"

Keep it simple, keep it sharp;
With blues guitar or angel's harp.
Who cares if the rhymes are carp?
It says "I love you."

And if the song's for girl or God;
And if the tune is old or odd;
And if they boo or perhaps applaud;
It has said "I love you."

And if I have a song to sing
To communicate my love.
I need my heart and soul and strength;
My mind is not enough.

I'm All Right, Jill

So maybe I'm looking a bit apprehensive.
So maybe I'm going back on the defensive;
But I'm all right, Jill. I'm all right.

So maybe my face acquires a sad expression.
So maybe I don't create the right impression;
But I'm all right, Jill. I'm all right.

You needn't worry, Jill.
You needn't worry about me.
I'm happy as I am;
I'm what I want to be.

So maybe I don't go out much or have good looks.
So maybe I'm no sportsman and prefer my books.
But I'm all right Jill. I'm all right.

So maybe I'm nobody; maybe I'm a jerk;
Maybe I'm unambitious about my work;
But I'm all right Jill. I'm all right.

So maybe I act childishly and immature
So maybe I don't know who I am - I'm not sure -
But I'm all right Jill. I'm all right.

So maybe I'm a little bit lonely and shy.
So maybe I'm afraid to look you in the eye.
But I'm all right Jill. I'm all right.

I'd Rather See You Smile

Save my jokes for a rainy day
When you might be needing a laugh;
And I'll only use really funny ones,
Sort the wheat out from the chaff.
I've been trying too hard to impress you
With my slick and humorous style.
Although I'd love to make you laugh,
I'd rather see you smile.

For when you smile
Your friends all smile with you.
You're like a child
And life is fun and new;
And when you smile I end up smiling too.

I'll send you poems when you're lonely;
When my words might make you less sad.
For when friends can suffer together
Then life isn't really so bad.
I'm trying too hard to impress you
With sad poems out of a file.
Although I'd gladly share your pain,
I'd rather see you smile.

That's Why I Like You

This is getting sentimental.
Girl, you are so kind and gentle
That it's not coincidental.
That's why I like you.
That's why I like you.

You would always pass inspection.
Outshine any art collection.
You'd win any by-election.
That's why I like you.
That's why I like you.

You are not big, you're elfin small.
You climb the heights without a fall.
You always dance you never crawl.
That's why I like you.
That's why I like you.

I think this will sound better sung.
It's not the best I've ever done.
I hope the tune and rhythm run.
Saying I like you.
Saying I like you.

You're sometimes here, you're sometimes there.
In troubles you're the first to share.
I'd like to see you everywhere.
That's why I like you.
That's why I like you.

Great Heart

Each club has got its colours.
Each team has got its mascot.
Each owner's got a racing coat
The jockey wears at Ascot;
But if I had to pick for you
A sign which I would use
To sum you up in pictures;
This is what I'd choose.

You're like a great heart
Beat beat beating like a drum;
Accompanying some singers singing
"We shall overcome."
Setting blood coursing
Through the corners of my mind.
Setting me in motion
Like a puppet which you wind.

Frozen Angels

The sculpture is
Silent in its beauty and strength
Reflecting the vision
Of the hands that have laboured;
But the image is static,
Immobile and dead;
The angel is frozen and cannot awake.

The painting is vivid,
Drawn with great skill.
Its background is chosen
To add to the wonder.
But the smile never varies;
The lips never kiss.
The angel is frozen and cannot awake.

The poem is clever -
A portrait in verse -
Revealing the poet's
Great love for the lady.
But she is invisible,
She can't be touched.
The angel is frozen and cannot awake.

But you are alive
And your parents were artists.
You are the creation
That was grown from their love.
Artists only follow
Where real angels lead them.
Art angels are frozen
And cannot awake.

Forgotten Someone?

Mum will get her favourite perfume; Dad will get a drill.
Brother Tom will get a sweater to keep out the chill.
Sister Sue will get some slippers; the twins will get some games;
And that I think is everyone - I'm running out of names.

Haven't you forgotten someone
Out of all that lot?
Surely you've forgotten someone,
Someone you should not.

Gran will get "The People's Friend" and Uncle Les "The Broons."
Pete will get his favourite treat - a box of macaroons.
Auntie Peg will get a handbag and Uncle Fred golf balls;
And that I think is everyone; there's no-one missed at all.

Bill will get some shaving lotion; Aunt Nan a box of chocs.
John will get a Star Wars game and Ruth a doll that talks.
Jane will get just what she wants - the new Coldplay CD;
And that I think is everyone - well done, my memory.

Ann will get a nice pink scarf and Jimmy's one is blue.
The postman gets an envelope; the binman gets one too.
The cat will get a wind-up mouse; the dog a special dish;
And that I think is everyone including the goldfish.

Early

Wrote this early morning,
Waiting for the dawn.
Somewhere life is ending,
But the children carry on.

Never used computer,
Preferred a fountain pen.
Times they were a-changin', Bob,
Now they will change again.

Many things stopped me writing;
Good things most of them.
Could be the time I'm thinking
For me to start again.

Carry on - yes we carry on,
Though there's fewer in the ark.
We swim against the tide of time;
Sandcastle dreams to make our mark.

Eleonora

Through a sea of blowing grass
On our daily walk we'd pass
Walking always hand in hand – hand in hand.
Telling poems to the river,
Looking forward to forever
We had the future planned - had it planned.

Eleanora Eleanora - I love you still,
Eleanora. I loved you then, and I swear I always will.

We lay in each other's arms
In the world of nature's charms
And we listened to the birds - Ah - the birds;
And the song they sang was sweet
But I cannot now repeat
For I do not know the words - know the words.

There was no tear in her eye
When she told me she would die;
So I shed enough tears for two - tears for two.
In acceptance of her fate
She was strong - as always great;
There was nothing we could do - we could do.

And when in her final hour
She lay with fading power,
Still she seemed to give out light - shining light;
While we watched our last sunset -
Just as on the day we met -
All too soon there came the night - endless night.

So I left I left the valley then;
I could not return again;
And I travelled far away - far away.
In this city now I dwell -
It's a slum suburb of hell.
I'm a madman people say - so they say.

Going

Night sneaks up from behind, planets shine.
Straggled cloud hangs, sad ragged twine.
Hurtling toward horizon, too much on my mind.
Leaving home.
Going home.

Speculation's the down-side of leaving
The "what ifs" and all the "might-have-beens."
Like this radio I'm not giving, just receiving
As I travel through this land of inbetween.

Country station playing, tenor whine;
Schmaltzy sad slow songs, same as mine;
Sentimental memories twist and twine.
Leaving home.
Going home.

Anticipation's the up-side of leaving;
The pregnant promise of what might be.
Something inside keeps me believing
That the best is still in front of me.

Lost in deep forest, a lonesome pine
Points to the secret heart of the great design.
Silent trees fall all the time
Leaving home.
Going home.

Barriers Down

You can't embrace in armour;
It's much more use for war.
You're wearing six inch plating
Can you tell me what that's for?
I've got my own protection
Should feelings come my way;
I'll make a silly joke
And try to laugh it all away.

Barriers down.
Barriers down.
Let's be honest with each other.
Barriers down.
Let's share our joy and pain together.

In sharing there is joy -
You know there's also pain.
The two are linked together
As Abel is to Cain.
But love will suffer longest
And it alone will last.
One day it will continue
When all the pain is past.

Divisions in the world -
It's always them and us.
So many wall-constructors
Who build on our mistrust.
We try to go our own way -
Our insularity.
That's no way to continue.
That's no way to break free.

The Canterbury Song

I sat within an ancient house,
An ancient house of Thine my God.
A building which had grown so old
In the service of the Lord.

Outside there was the carolling
Of a Sally Army band,
Reminding us of the season,
Bringing good news to the land.

Sing sing hallelujah - Praise the Lord for Christmas Day.
Glory glory hallelu - Give thanks today

Two thousand years of newness
Springing from that baby's birth;
For that day in Bethlehem
Christ joined us on the earth.

I marveled at the contrast there -
The age of You the timeless one,
And the newness of that baby's birth
And our new birth in Your Son.

Now this house has grown so old;
So many pilgrims passed this way -
A cavalcade of faithful ones
Down to the present day.

Christmas is not out of date
For it is both old and new;
For upon that special day
Christ came to earth for me and you.

Brenda's Song (Don't Call Me Muriel)

Don't call me Muriel -
That is not my name.
My homeland is occupied;
That is why I came;
And now you seek to stifle
My personality;
Calling me a name not mine -
A name that isn't me.

Don't call me, Don't call me Don't call me Muriel.
Don't call me. Don't call me. That is not my name.

I've been sent so far away -
A refugee of war.
I know that others in this world
Are suffering much more.
It's not my choice that I am here,
This bleak and lonely place.
I'd give so much for just one hug
Or e'en a smiling face.

At least I don't have to fear
The footsteps in the night.
The sense of growing horror
Without a chance of flight;
But this is such a desert,
A dismal place to be,
The sense of dislocation
Of no longer being me.

My name is Brenda!

Baked Beans

Isn't it such a pity
To rush in from the city,
Going to a meeting
Without much time for eating;
So I open up a tin and there I find within
A rare delicacy for me to eat for tea.
There's a lot of goodness in it
I'll heat it up just for minutes
While exchanging suit for jeans
Then I'll go and eat my beans
In the kitchen.

*If you are what you eat
Then you'd better be discrete
About baked beans.*

In this manic modern world
When your poor head gets whirled,
The important thing is speed;
That's true even when you feed.
You don't go by what is good
When you choose your food
Instead you look for what's quick
Hoping it won't make you sick.
Though not really the in thing
There's a million housewives sing
And we all know what that means -
Another plate of beans
For you at teatime.

Far better when the food is
More like a forbidden fruit;
So rarely do you eat them
And then only for a treat.
The extractor fan turned on
Until the smell is gone.
It's a source of some dismay
That your dad's a true gourmet
And we all know what that means;
You've not had many beans
In your childhood.

The Tide is Turning

A new generation
Is learning to praise
The God of their fathers -
Unchanging His ways.
Who gives life it's meaning
Who gives life it's zing.
C'mon everybody
Join in and sing.
Hearts are burning.
The tide is turning.
Hallelujah!
They're coming home!

When you're in Jesus you're never alone.
It's time to get out of
Your comfort zone.
Follow the Leader
Wherever He says
And you will know joy
Through all of your days.
Hearts are burning.
The tide is turning.
Hallelujah!
We're coming home!

Stand Your Ground

When the last place you want to be is here
And you wish that you could simply disappear
And you're feeling sick with stomach-churning fear -
That's the time to stand your ground.

When life seems tougher than it was yesterday
Or you can't find a single word to say
Or you want to cry and then run away -
That's the time to stand your ground.

Stand your ground stand up for Him.
He stood His ground for you.
Don't be afraid -
You're not alone -
He will help you through.

When others laugh or sneer or spit
Or make you feel a hypocrite;
And you plan to retreat - a little bit -
That's the time to stand your ground.

When He brings victory from each defeat;
When He says your life is now complete
And you must face the Judgement Seat -
That's the time you'll stand your ground.

Cities of the Plain

I'll tap dance on your ballet shoes and whistle at your gale.
Forsake the days of idle waste and admit that I've failed.
I'll crack away the outer shell to show the seed inside.
Truth revealed, the future sealed.
There's no place left to hide.

With the turning of a card I'll choose the way to go
Before I set too hard to let emotion show.
Hopes rise first - then drift away - and, like them, I cannot stay;
Like the Cities of the Plain, I'll not be seen again.

I'll visit aging fascists and I'll wear a party hat.
I'll drink strong beer with all good cheer and maybe I'll grow fat.
I'll act a little strangely so they can't rely on me
To be a sport – jolly good sort –
And they'll have to set me free.

I don't like the scenery; I don't fit in at all.
I'll disappear like the passing year past the point of no recall.
I must escape from all this. This is no way to go on.
A moment's pain, Cities of the Plain
Were instantly forever gone.

Inside Out

Inside out and outside in
Have no doubts – enquire within.
The Lord He says "Now follow me
And I will set you free."

Everybody's got the weight of the world
Pressing on their shoulders so hard.
The Lord will lift it if we just ask Him;
It's only pride that keeps us apart.

Inside – sometimes we feel unhappy
But no-one seems to know or care.
The Lord – He sees deep inside us
And all our troubles he will bear;
All our troubles He will bear.

Outside – sometimes we're offensive;
We try to scare the world away.
The Lord – He just won't be put off
And He wants us to follow His way.
He wants us to follow His Way.

Songs from the Heart

There's songs of celebration.
There's songs about defeat.
There's songs about the flashing eyes
Of the girl you'd like to meet.
There's songs about your mother and
There's songs about your dad.
There's songs about experiences
You wish you'd never had.

Songs from the heart just give me
Songs from the heart.
My favourite kind of songs are
Songs from the heart.
The lasting type of songs are
Songs from the heart.
Songs from the heart just give me
Songs from the heart.

There's songs about the earth
There's songs about the sky.
There's songs about the reasons
Little children have to die.
There's songs about your pains and
There's songs about your joys.
There's songs about girls
And there's songs about boys.

There's songs of sound and fury
There's songs that say much less.
There's songs of snatching failure
From the wide jaws of success.

There's songs of peaceful waters
There's songs about the shade.
There's songs about the borrowed grave
In which your friend was laid.

There's songs about romantic love.
There's songs about fun sex.
There's songs that have a surface
But an underlying text.
There's songs that make you cry and
There's songs that make you laugh.
There's songs about wheat and
Its difference from chaff.

There's songs that make you think and
There's songs that make you smile.
There's songs that keep your fears at bay
For just a little while.
There's songs of absolution.
There's songs about our guilt.
There's songs that are better sung
By a Scotsman in a kilt.

There's songs with inspiration
There's songs that it passed by.
There's songs that ask the question
But cannot tell you why.
There's songs that are so empty
There's songs that are so full.
There's songs that do not rhyme
Though that's the general rule.

A Hundred Million Starving Christs

A hundred million starving Christs
Hold out their hands to me
While I stand, mute and helpless,
And thinking of my tea.

Sorry , Lord, I passed you by.
Sorry, Lord, you know I try;
And so, until the day I die,
I'll try to serve you better -
Love you more.

A lost and lonely Son of God
Is asking me for something;
But I've no time to get involved
With other matters pressing.

A bleeding, bevvied, Son of God
Lay bleeding on my way.
I'll phone for help when I get home;
Well, what else could I say?

Sleeping Beauty in Reverse

Well I woke up this morning with a ringing in my ears.
It wasn't my alarm clock; the sound was not that near.
And I stumbled to the telephone with the sleep still in my eyes.
I picked up the receiver - it was such a nice surprise;
For it was you was calling. I'd wondered if you would.
My heart was beating fast and I was feeling good.

Wake up, Steeping Beauty in reverse.
Shake up, hear that phone a ringing.
Wake up. It must be the princess.
Wake up, Sleeping Beauty in reverse.

You'd been away for ages - but you were back a week.
I thought you wouldn't call me; I was feeling rather weak.
But then on Thursday morning, when the week was almost past,
My telephone was ringing and my heart was beating fast.
It was so good to hear your voice while I wasn't quite awake.
It's really more like dreaming; but a lovely way to wake.

I tried to write a third verse but the words just would not come.
Had I lost my writing touch? Or else been stricken dumb?
It isn't very easy to say how I felt that day.
I'd like to keep that moment just in case it slips away.
This is saying nothing; It's the usual surplus verse.
But it was like a fairy tale - Sleeping Beauty in reverse.

Black Dog's Back

Black dog's back,
Biting at my heels again.
Black dog's back,
Biting at my heels again.
I can hardly feel
Through the half-healed weals.
Black dog's back,
Biting at my heels again.

Clouds roll in
Hiding the sun from sight.
Clouds roll in
Hiding the sun from sight.
I know it's there
I just don't care.
Clouds roll in
Hiding the sun from sight.

No energy;
I do what I can to get by.
No energy;
I do what I can to get by.
I'm a hopeless case;
A waste of space.
No energy;
I do what I can to get by.

Acceptance

The lonely one will find a friend.
The hurting one need not pretend.
The broken one will be restored.
The needy one won't be ignored.

So let us strive that this might be,
Accepting all that need set free.
For this our love must be sincere
Let's work to bring His Kingdom near.

Let none who come be turned away;
Open our ears to what they say
And earn the right for us to share
The Good News that is here not there.

The captive ones will be set free
From chains that ruin their liberty;
And then we too will freedom know
Following Him who tells us so.

So let us not presume to judge
With flint-like hearts that will not budge
Be open to the Spirit's flow
And by our love let people know.

For all are equal in God's eyes
This is the day to realise.
New life will grow - but when Lord when?
The Good News that is now not then.

New Beginnings

Sing a song of new beginnings; the hope that springs each day.
Sing a song of new beginnings - along the ever changing way.

When unknown angels entertain us
In a reversal of the norm.
When the rain beats down outside
And we have shelter from the storm.
When the night is cold and dreary,
The stranger's spare bed is warm.
Life provides another milestone -
Not a tickbox on some form.

From His treasure store of riches
We cannot accept enough
Of what we know really matters
And not just things and stuff.
The gifts that are chosen for us
Fit like hands inside a glove.
In the presents there is plenty
In the presence there is love.

When there's darkness in and round us
Seeming more than we can cope.
Though the twilight time has died
Yet there always remains hope.
There's no need to feel defeated
Or sit around and mump and mope.
From the pit we're pulled to safety;
His the strong hand on the rope.

Living for each passing moment
Calm acceptance like a cat.
Of what can seem truly random -
A name drawn from a hat.
There's so much we don't know
Lifelong learning isn't flat.
But we know this - we are loved
We can be sure of that.

Let us cross one final ocean
To explore the Promised Land.
Tearful partings, joyful meetings.
We begin to understand.
One who loves us holds and keeps us
In the hollow of His hand.
When we see the bigger picture
We will know He had it planned.

Those who went this way before us
And those whom we've yet to meet.
Those who keep the home fires burning
And those with highway feet.
There's always somewhere to explore;
Google's not made it obsolete.
Our adventure's never over until it is complete.

The recurring colour purple;
The royal colour of a king.
On the outer edge of rainbows -
Those arcs that promise bring.
Markings on a sheet of music
The notes that we should sing.
For a love song to our Father
The gifts that wise folk bring.

Notes on Individual Songs

Pointing at the Pachyderm   (page 8)
No music yet.

One of the most recent items included and the "title "track". (Well almost – the song is singular and the book is plural).   It arose out of an E-mail correspondence with my friend from the Scottish Fellowship of Christian Writers, Rachel Chown.   She was riddled with cancer and went home from her beloved Dundee to her parents' house in Essex for her final months.   In an email I awkwardly broached the subject of mentioning the unmentionable.   To which Rachel came back telling me please to use words such as "cancer" and "death" since she was fed up with people avoiding them.

I replied to the effect that this was probably just as well as I was constitutionally unable to avoid drawing attention to the elephant in the room and was in fact the sort of person who "pointed at the pachyderm".   I was taken with the phrase – which I don't think I had ever heard before - and wrote the lines based on it and shared them with Rachel who enjoyed them.

Rachel was a wonderful person who had a photographer's eye as a poet and a poet's sensibilities as a photographer.   I am not the only person who misses her greatly.

Jacob's Well (page 10)
No music yet.

One of my favourite Bible passages is the strange encounter between Jesus and the woman at the well.   Among many other points of significance, the number of taboos and social barriers

106

which Jesus subverted was remarkable. Why doesn't His church always act the same way?

(Don't You Remember) The Belvederes? (page 12)
Music by Elaine McGregor.

My daughter had got a keyboard when she was about thirteen and put the music to this.

There is a vogue for tribute bands and also some continuing bands (The Who, The Rolling Stones) seem essentially to have become their own tribute bands. I think that thought was in the back of my mind when I came up with this recollection of a band which never in fact existed.

To the best of my knowledge, there never was an album called "Walsingham"; and "Salisbury Gears" was a deliberate mashing of "Disraeli Gears" by Cream and "Salisbury" by Uriah Heep.

I was reading one of the "His Dark Materials" by Phillip Pullman at the time. (Not all Christians dislike this marvellous trilogy as a matter of principle). The next chapter I read after coming up with the name "The Belvederes" was called "The Belvedere." I like "coincidences".

I recently discovered that there actually was a band called "The Belvederes" – I found one track by them on Napster – "He's a Square". It's on "32 Original Historic Rockabilly Classics Vol 4". It has a very similar tune to "Johnny B Goode". (See the note below about "Horoscope Blues".)

Dead Man (page 14)
Music by Ian McGregor.

Based on a conversation with Marjorie Brown about her reaction when her husband, Ken, became a Christian. She thought this was truly bizarre on his part. She later "saw the light" in both senses.

Adrenaline and Grace (page 16)
Music by Ian McGregor.

One of the best sermons I ever heard was by Julyan Lidstone at Queens Park Baptist Church. While it was a sermon, at times it veered towards being a one man play about Jeremiah. He preached mainly in character as Jeremiah and it was amazing. I overheard him afterwards saying that he had written this on the plane home from one of the former Soviet republics and he was so tired he was "running on adrenaline and grace". What a phrase! And with the subject matter of Jeremiah planted in my mind, this song followed soon after.

Stuck Inside of Drumcree (with the Garvaghy Blues Again) (page 17)
Music by me – although really it was by Bob Dylan.

The title is a clear nod to Dylan's "Stuck Inside of Mobile (With the Memphis Blues Again"). However, having "borrowed" the format of the title, I ended up "borrowing" the tune as well.

The song was about the recurring stand-off in the Northern Ireland marching season where an Orange walk wanted to go through a mainly Nationalist area and is in itself yet another variant on the Romeo and Juliet story.

It was some time after this was written that I realised that I had rhymed "again" with "again" in the first verse. However, rather than going back and changing it I realised that I had accidentally stressed the message of the verse – about history repeating itself – by rhyming a word with itself. If you thought that was a clever literary device – please ignore the previous sentence!

Europa Hotel (page 18)
Music by Ian McGregor.

I nearly moved to Belfast when I was 6 or 7. My father worked in the Clyde shipyards. From school, he went into the drawing office of A & J Inglis at Pointhouse (the site of the new Transport Museum) and, among other ships, designed the Waverley. Inglis closed in about 1962 and he moved to the Glasgow yard of Harland & Wolff who owned Inglis. Harland & Wolff then closed on the Clyde and he was offered a job in their Belfast yard - which he nearly took - but he and my mother decided to stay in Glasgow. This was before the start of the "Troubles" and, more significantly for us, was not all that long before he got cancer and died (on April Fool's Day, 1967).

I finally made it to Belfast in about 1996 on a day trip with my older son, Stuart. It rained the whole time! At one point we were waiting at a bus stop when I realised we were opposite the Europa Hotel which was bombed on many occasions in the past. I have rarely been so glad when a bus turned up!

I Don't Do Flowers (page 19)
Music by Ian McGregor

The love of my life, and wife of over 30 years, Carole (happily, both the same person!) is curiously under-represented in this collection. This is in fact the only song that is directly for her. It was an explanation of why, although I hope I am as romantic as the next Scotsman (which admittedly is not setting the bar very high!) I don't "do" flowers. I think we are now up to four bunches in over 30 years.

To be fair, I did write a lot of poems for her.

Fluffy Dice (page 20)
Music by Ian McGregor

This started from a feeling of helplessness in the face of need. A friend, Ian Smith (*illustrator extraordinaire* - please see the cover of this book), shared about meeting a man who was living in a car and buying him a fish supper.

I made a rather shabby comment about buying fluffy dice for the car. This song is an extension of that idea. "Dice" turned out to be a great word for rhyming.

The Frail Broken Children of Dust (page 22)
Music by Ian McGregor.

An attempt to empathise with a friend who was going through a **very** bad time.

John Prine Derivative New Home Moving Blues (page 24)
Music by Ian McGregor.

A friend and colleague, Stephen Vance, was moving house. He was, and is, also a great fan of John Prine. Hence the song.

The Year of Jubilee (page 25)
Music by Ian McGregor (although I have forgotten it - so time to start again).

A setting of the words of Isaiah quoted by Jesus at the start of His ministry.

Judge Puffenberger (page 26)
Music by Ian McGregor.

Ellie is a friend of ours from Toledo, Ohio, whom Carole met on the Internet and who subsequently visited us.

She subsequently got married to Donald and the wedding was conducted by - Judge Puffenberger! This was a song for them.

Going to the Lebanon (page 27)
Music by David Barron.

A group of young people from Queens Park Baptist Church were going on a trip to the Lebanon. This included my daughter, Elaine, and David's oldest son, Jonathan. This song was written for their send off service. As it happened, Elaine ended up not going. When she later on went on a mission trip it was four years later when she was seventeen. She was living on the border between Moss Side and Trafford Park in Manchester (which would have given Beirut a run for its money).

Magdalene Falls (page 28)
No music as yet.

I have written quite a few sketches and monologues about Bible events seen from an unusual perspective. This song is in that genre.

Noah's Got the Blues Again (page 30)
Music by Ian McGregor.

Rather following on from the above. Essentially, the thought behind this was that Noah, as well as thankfulness for the saving of his family, would also be prone to more negative reactions to the Flood. Post Traumatic Stress Disorder?

No Pain Like His (page 31)
Music by Ian McGregor. (Although it is probably a bit close to Bryn Haworth's wonderful "What kind of love is this?" so probably ripe for a new tune).

Jesus turns up in many of these lyrics. This goes some way to explaining why.

Outrage (page 32)
No music as yet. A response to the nail bombing of a gay pub in, I think, London.

Shadow of Death (page 33)
Music by Ian McGregor.

One of my favourites and written after a day out with my younger son, David, when he was about seven. He liked the idea of being in a song!

The "Shadow of Death" in the song is literal as well as metaphorical. We had been at M & D at Strathclyde Park and were heading across towards Hamilton. We passed through the shadow of the Duke of Hamilton's Mausoleum.

I have subsequently acquired a CD recorded inside the Mausoleum which reputedly has the longest echo in a man-made structure in the world. "Into Silence" by Tommy Smith is just him playing saxophone inside the building. Beautiful.

She Tempted Me (Blues for Bathsheba) (page 34)
Music by Ian McGregor.

A take on the adultery between King David and Bathsheba. Partly in the light of Bono describing the Psalms as containing the blues. Leonard Cohen's "Hallelujah" was around long before then but I didn't love that as much as I do now - although I suspect it informed my song a bit. When David wrote about this in the Psalms he did not attempt to justify himself as he does in this song.

The Love that Bleeds (page 35)
No music as yet. This would need a bit of a rewrite to fit a tune because the line lengths differ widely.

Christmastime is Coming (page 36)
No music as yet, despite several attempts.

Written for a Christmas Watchnight service. There was a bit of a debate in the drama group about whether we could say "crap" in a service. We thought that, if we used it, we might not get asked again. We did – and we didn't!

Spirit is Willing (page 38)
Music by Ian McGregor.

I can't remember the context of writing this. I think it may have been following on from someone's observation that many worship songs are from the "I" perspective.

As We Baptise (page 39)
Music – "In Praise of Islay".

The first (in this book) of a series of hymns. This was written when I stumbled on the tune which I had never heard of.

What She Could (page 40)
Music – "The Water is Wide".

Written for an Easter week service. My wife, Carole, was speaking about the woman who broke the alabaster jar of expensive perfume and anointed the feet of Jesus who commented that "she did what she could". At first sight this does not seem to be saying much – but it actually says a lot; what more could she, or anyone else, do?

Calypso Hosanna (page 41)
Music – "Calypso Carol".

At our church we have the opportunity for people to choose a favourite hymn for inclusion in a service. Someone new chose the "Calypso Carol" as being one her favourites. We wanted to affirm her choice. However, the only problem was that the service in question was "Palm Sunday" and a carol didn't quite fit in! "Don't worry" I said, rather rashly, "I can write some new words to the tune".

A nice example of someone accidentally commissioning a piece of writing!

Harvest Hymn (page 42)
Music – "We plough the fields and scatter"

This is the odd one out of all the lyrics here. I have actually made money from it! I won £30 in a hymn writing competition run by the Scottish Fellowship of Christian Writers. (www.sfcw.info). It is one of my favourite tunes and this was actually the third set of lyrics I have written for it. This is the only one included in this book. The others are in the walk-in cupboard!

Coming Home (page 43)
Music by Ian McGregor

This was written for a home coming service at South Shawlands in the Homecoming Scotland Year of 2009. Based on the most famous homecoming in the Bible – that of the Prodigal Son.

I wisely got someone else to sing this and the only public performance (to date) of this song was brought to life by Sue Clist.

New Songs (page 44)
Music – "The hand O God has guided".

I have recently been consciously aiming to write contemporary hymns in a traditional format. This is both an example and an exploration of that.

The Wounds Are Still There (page 45)
Music by Dougie Nicol.

Some time ago, Dougie and I were at a service at Glasgow Westend Vineyard. The sermon was preached by Billy Kent who was, at the time, their assistant pastor. The sermon was excellent and both inspired and informed these words.

Joy (page 46)
Music by Beethoven. The "Ode to Joy" from his 9th Symphony.

Every lyric I write after this will have an inferior tune!

In the Kingdom (page 47)
Music – "The Work of the Weavers" better known as "The Welly Boot Song".

Written for a children's talk at Priesthill & Nitshill Church in 2011. I had tried several times over more than 20 years to write

new words to this tune. Finally it worked. (I hope you agree!).
To be honest, I don't know if my granny ever said "Many a mickle
mak's a muckle". However, it is the sort of thing she would have
said, and I know my mother said something of the kind though
perhaps not in those words. "Take care of the pennies and the
pounds will take care of themselves."

Fruit Trees (page 48)
Music – "Rowan Tree."

Written for a service on the fruit of the Spirit. I came across
the song "Rowan Tree" sung by my friend, Heather Innes, loved
it and wrote the words while listening to it on repeat.

Heather deserves another mention for inadvertently kick
starting the process of pulling this book together. I had the
privilege of giving her a little help and encouragement in getting
her lovely book "New Beginnings" ready for publication. This
helped create the momentum for doing this.

Centenary Hymn (page 49)
Music – "Sine Nomine" by Ralph Vaughan Williams

I have been part of three centenary celebrations for Church of
Scotland congregation; two congregations – three centenaries!
This was written for the centenary celebrations of South
Shawlands.

If Christ Be Not Raised Up (page 50)
Music – "To God be the Glory"

Entered in the same competition as "Harvest Hymn" above. It was written for a short service at which the passage on which this is based was being preached on.

We Can Count on You (page 51)
Music and about half of the words by Dougie Nicol.

I woke up (the morning!) after one of Dougie's sermons with the phrase "We can count on You" in mind and the idea of following through numbers. Dougie took this and changed (improved!) and added some the words. This was the first song we had written together for 27 years!

Been There, Done That, Worn the Crown of Thorns (page 52)
Music by Ian McGregor.

Another unique song in that words and music were written at the same time.

The first (of two) public performances of this (to date) was at an Easter event in Queens Park Baptist Church. Again wisely I got someone else to sing it, Callum Tooth, and suggested that he be accompanied by James Conn on saxophone. It was a marvellous performance, which sadly was not recorded. As I wrote to Callum and James afterwards thanking them, I had no idea I had written such a good song.

Main Street (page 53)
Music by Ian McGregor.

This was written for an event in Neilston. The person who invited the drama group I was in gave us some very helpful and honest feedback. He referred to this song as having very good words and that those who could make them out really appreciated them! On this occasion, I had unwisely not got someone else to sing them!

Without Siobhan (page 54)
No music yet.

Siobhan was the name of the still born daughter of a colleague's sister. This song is not specifically about that although it was partly informed by that.

Working Granny (page 55)
Music by Ian McGregor.

A response to "Working Mother" written by Martyn Joseph and Stewart Henderson. A sad and angry song about a single mother forced into prostitution. This is intended to be sadder but with a grim humour imparted by the narrator being a boy of about eight.

Paint Yer Bollards (page 56)
No music as yet.

Another product of that trip to Belfast with Stuart (see notes on "Europa Hotel" above).

Seeded by the red, white and blue painted kerbs in East Belfast within site of the cranes of Harland & Wolff.

Living Black & White (page 57)
Music – "Passing Through."

Based on a lively debate in the drama group about the merits of some magazine photos of Gail Porter.

Horoscope Blues (page 58)
Music by Ian McGregor (kind of).

This was the first song I wrote after learning guitar. Basic 12 bar blues progression – I lifted it from Larry Norman's "Let the Tape Keep Rolling" which he lifted from Chuck Berry's "Johnny B Goode".

Days Gone By (page 59)
No music yet.

Can there be any happy songs that start with a variation "woke up this morning?" I don't always feel like this.

The Victor (page 60)
No music as yet.

Written for a very good friend (Raymond Muirhead) when he was dying. I know he read it and I dare to hope he drew some comfort from it.

Call God (page 62)
Music by Ian McGregor.

Based on a conversation with my friend, John Wallace. He was talking about having prayed in distinctly non-religious language. I admired the honesty and have to admit having done the same.

Across the Decades (page 64)
Music by Ian McGregor.

Written for the centenary show at South Shawlands (see "Centenary Hymn" above).

The show contained music from the ten decades of that century. The song was written for this. It was not the musical highpoint of the evening but it was the only mention Jesus got so I think I did something right.

The show was on for two nights. I had a haircut and a beard shearing in between the two nights and changed the key. My apologies to anyone who was trying to splice together videos of the two evenings!

O Little Town of Bethlehem 2 (page 66)
Music – "O Little Town of Bethlehem"

Always one of my favourite carols. I was saddened by the continuing tension in the Holy Land and particularly in Bethlehem and wrote these words during a train journey.

Caring (page 68)
No music as yet.

"Infect" was a strange word and I struggled for an alternative. Eventually I decided that it said what I wanted to say so I left it.

The Routes of Coincidence (page 69)
Music by Dougie Nicol.

At the time this was written (late 70s) I had been reading a few of Arthur Koestler's books including "The Roots of Coincidence". I was reading one of his book, "Janus", on the bus to work. When I arrived, I was introduced to a new colleague – Janusz!

Burning Bridges (page 70)
Music by Dougie Nicol.

This was written for a farewell show at Cathcart South Church Youth Fellowship just before Dougie left Glasgow and accountancy to become a postman in Aberdeenshire and then to explore his call to the ministry. Mention should be made of Peter Gabriel's "A Wonderful Day in a One Way World" as the source of the "one way world" phrase in the song.

Past and Future Echo (page 71)
Music by Dougie Nicol.

Not really sure what this was about. What is was **not** about was a pregnancy. The title is an echo of "The One and Future King" by T H White.

Pinstripe Gypsy (page 72)
Music by Dougie Nicol.

As mentioned above, Dougie and I were accountants together. This song was about what he left behind! In those days I travelled about a lot more than I do now. "Gypsy" wasn't a politically incorrect term in those days and in fact I always thought of it as being slightly exotic and romantic. Mention should be made of Pete Townshend's song "Going Mobile" on "Who's Next" which contained the phrase "I'm an air-conditioned gypsy".

Chameleons (page 74)
Music by Dougie Nicol.

One of several songs written with Dougie about non communication. I love chameleons; the bad taste but funny joke about putting a chameleon on a tartan travelling rug and it exploding; and I like being a slightly perverse chameleon and not quite blending in.

Pierced (page 75)
Music by Peter Bloomfield.

One of two songs written with Peter for that Easter presentation at Queens Park Baptist Church. (See comments above on "Been There, Done That, Worn the Crown of Thorns.)" In connection with this presentation by Arc Theatre Company I had contacted several of the worship leaders to be involved. Callum Tooth was one of these, as was Nikki Meek. In responding, she pointed out that she would be 9 months pregnant by the time of the event. My initial thought was that it was a pity this wasn't a Christmas presentation! However, my second thought was that Mary was very much present to see and suffer through the events of Easter. Hence the song – beautifully sung by Nikki and accompanied by Peter.

It was a couple of years later that, in a church in Germany, I say a statue of Mary with several daggers sticking into her. Even with the insights provided by writing the lyrics it was a bit bizarre but fantastically evocative.

It Should've Been Me (page 76)
Music by Peter Bloomfield.

This is the second of the songs referred to above. This time it was about Barabbas and was sung by Peter to his own backing track. We should have written more songs together – maybe one day.

Leaving "I Love You" (page 78)
No music yet.

Not sure where this one came from.

I'm All Right Jill (page 79)
Tune by Dougie Nicol.

As mentioned above I went to a boys' only school which didn't do a lot for my confidence in speaking to girls. When this was written (summer of 1980?) the barriers were starting to come down. I think this was partly based on a conversation with a (female) colleague (not called Jill) at a residential training course.

The title is an obvious play on "I'm all right, Jack".

I'd Rather See You Smile (page 80)
Music by Dougie Nicol.

One of a number of (my) unrequited love songs.

That's Why I Like You (page 81)
Music by Dougie Nicol.

Unrequited.

Great Heart (page 82)
Music by Dougie Nicol

And again! One of our best songs – sadly it is only 42 seconds long because I couldn't come up with a second verse.

Frozen Angels (page 83)
Music by Dougie Nicol.

This is another unique one. As mention in the introduction, only one item doesn't rhyme. This is it.

Forgotten Someone? (page 84)
Music – "Putting on the Style."

Written for a Christmas show. Or should that by Xmas show - if you want a clue as to Who is missing! The CD keeps getting updated; I think it was an LP in the original lyric.

Early (page 85)
No music as yet.

This was the first thing I had written for a long time. It was written in the strange calm hour or so between Carole leaving for the Prince & Princess of Wales Hospice where her father was dying and me waking the children for school.

Eleanora (page 86)
Music by Dougie Nicol.

A sublimated unrequited love song. It is based on a story by Edgar Allen Poe. (I think it is the same one as "Lady Eleanor" by Alan Hull of Lindisfarne. He was another big influence – the first lyric I wrote was new words to "The Fog on the Tyne.") It was performed by Dougie at a folk club in Aberdeenshire on the same night that Dave Swarbrick appeared there.

Going (page 88)
Music by Ian McGregor. Words jointly with Sybil Maguire.

One of my favourite songwriters is the Canadian Bruce Cockburn. I was on a newsgroup for him during my early days online and had the idea of reaching out to anyone on the list who was a song writer and interested in a possible collaboration. This was the outcome of this. Sybil Maguire was a music journalist from New Jersey and also a lyricist. (I was actually looking for a music writer! By which I mean a writer of music.) We decided to try writing alternate lines, which we did, and then I think I added the chorus and put a tune to it. Unsurprisingly, it displays a heavy Bruce Cockburn influence.

Barriers Down (page 89)
Music by Dougie Nicol.

Another of these non communication songs written with Dougie. This kind of followed on from a Youth Fellowship conference song which he wrote, called "Barriers".

The Canterbury Song (page 90)
Music by Dougie Nicol.

One of my first trips away from home in my days as a "pinstripe Gypsy" (see above) was in December 1976 to Ashford in Kent. On the Saturday in the middle of the trip I went to Canterbury and wrote these words inside the Cathedral. Several years later they became a song.

Brenda's Song (Don't Call Me Muriel) (page 91)
Music by Helen Macalan.

I was privileged to hear the story of Brenda Bisson who was an evacuee from Guernsey to Glasgow during the Second World War. She had good experiences in Glasgow and her family left behind survived the war so the story had a happy ending.

However, her first billet was in London with an odd and undemonstrative family. Very sad for a little girl of seven who had been taken away from her family at very short notice – hugs were not on offer. But stranger still; the family had a daughter of their own, also called Brenda. So they decreed that evacuee Brenda was to be called Muriel.

Brenda very kindly gave her permission for her story to be reflected in this song.

The music and the definitive performance of this song is by my friend, Helen Macalan, who lives on the Royal Mile in Edinburgh. (Not exactly "on" – she stays in a flat.) Helen rightly pointed out that "Brenda's Song" was a much more appropriate title.

Baked Beans (page 92)
Music by Dougie Nicol.

I haven't had many friends who have been offspring of the minor nobility. However, she claimed that her father had been very disapproving of baked beans. Hence this song.

If anyone reading this can identify the source of the words in the chorus:

> *If you are what you eat*
> *You'd better be discrete*
> *About baked beans.*

please let me know. I would love them to be original but I suspect that they might not be. I have tried and failed to trace them. If you don't recognise them, remember where you saw them first!

The Tide is Turning (page 94)
No music yet.

In 2002 I was asked to do some drama workshops at a youth weekend from Queens Park Baptist Church. It was a great weekend although there was limited uptake on the drama. However, there was a creative buzz about the weekend and I came up with two lyrics and a sketch. This is the first lyric.

Stand Your Ground (page 95)
No music yet.

This is the second lyric from that weekend.

Cities of the Plain (page 96)
Music by Dougie Nicol and Ian McGregor

This was our "punk" song. The lyrics are remarkably negative and I don't remember feeling that bad at the time so maybe I was using my imagination.

Inside Out (page 97)
Music and half of lyrics by Dougie Nicol.

This was the theme song for a youth fellowships conference in 1978. It was one of the first songs we wrote together.

The words of the chorus were written in a bus home from Glasgow City Centre on the back of the till receipt for "Give 'Em Enough Rope" the second LP by The Clash.

Songs from the Heart (page 98)
No music yet.

This was an attempt at a theme song for a songwriting event at Queens Park Baptist Church. It was organised by Raymond Muirhead (see notes on "The Victor"). It didn't work then as a song.

The three songs I sang at the even were "Fluffy Dice", "Been There, Done That, Worn the Crown of Thorns" and "Adrenaline and Grace".

A Hundred Million Starving Christs (page 100)
Music by Ronnie Blair (RIP).

This was one of three songs I wrote with Ronnie although these words existed as a poem for some years before I gave them to him.

The most challenging words in the Bible may well be Jesus saying "whatever you do for the least of these, you also do for me" and vice versa.

Sleeping Beauty in Reverse (page 101)
Music by Dougie Nicol.

Another one of the unrequited love songs. Although, just for a few hours one Thursday, I thought it was maybe going to be requited. I am glad it wasn't – God had something very much better in store for me!

Black Dog's Back (page 102)
Music by Ian McGregor

Depression has been a part of my life for most of the period covered by these lyrics. Some of them are because of depression. Some of them are despite depression. This one is about depression.

Acceptance (page 103)
Music "O Tannenbaum" (the German Carol) or "The Red Flag" (the German Karl).

Sometimes when you are depressed, being accepted is very important. This should happen in church. Sometimes it does.

New Beginnings (page 104)
Music by Jacynth Hamill.

This ran "pachyderm" close as the first item. However, the title is also the title of a recently published book by one of my many friends from the Scottish Fellowship of Christian Writers, Heather Innes. This is part autobiography and part anthology. I was delighted to have the opportunity of giving Heather some encouragement and a little assistance in bringing this to publication.

It also broke the ground for this collection since it showed me how relatively easy the process of publication was using a combination of Lulu and Kindle.

The words draw on themes and incidents in the book and the music is by Heather's partner in the singing group, Caim.

131

It seems best to end this collection with a song about new beginnings.

Afterword (Running Order)

Given how much attention I have given to running orders in the past it is strange that I have not tried to sequence the items in this book. The reason for this is that I considered it but couldn't decide how to structure it. I could have partially split it into types of songs, or collaborators, or approximately chronological order. Instead I left it as it came which means that there are "clusters". I did a bit of shuffling to ensure that lyrics which ran to two pages appeared on facing pages.